Rune Magick

The Use of Runes as Magickal Tools for Simple Magickal Workings

Keith Morgan

ISBN 1-872189-55-5

Mandrake Press Ltd.
Essex House, Thame
Oxon. OX9 3LS
ENGLAND

Contents

About the Author

KEITH MORGAN was born in Cheshire in 1961. He studied various Occult teachings from the age of 11 and was initiated into the craft of the wise in 1977.

He continues to work as a practising High Priest of Wicca, and as a publisher and author in many esoteric fields. He writes in a simple and concise style which is easily understood by both the initiate and the student of the occult arts.

Keith is proud and outspoken about his beliefs, he has given interviews on local and national TV and radio and continues to be in the forefront of developing new ideas about all Occult teachings and paths.

Anna Greenwood

introduction

In the natural world of magick, there are many symbols and signs of power. They are natural elements that we can harness in creating a magick of our own, for what we are doing is enhancing the very power that we all possess with natural symbols of power.

Runes are such symbols of power, for they in their smallest form, often as little as but one line, depict a natural power or source of power that mankind can learn from, use within magick and benefit from. The power that runes contain can be put to use in many magickal ways; they can be used as a divination aid, as a power to invoke or banish, as a power to link the subconscious psyche into a greater energy force, that of the different components of the natural world.

All this and more is possible through a simple symbol! This is not a subject of the impossible, this is magick, and true powerful magick at that. With the symbols of the runes we can be taken onto Otherworld journeys, we can journey within ourselves, we can venture into realms of unknown possibilities. Runes are the key and our guide to mysterious worlds, all of which we have within ourselves. Upon our sacred journeys we will not be travelling many miles but through time and space, back to a time when the Wise Ones of the tribe were respected, when what they had to say was listened to; we are going back to that time; we will be talking to those ancient ancestors all of whom are very much alive and with us today — they live through their magick, they live through the runes.

Take this as your opportunity to journey into the underworld, to follow in the footsteps of Odin on his quest for knowledge, take the challenge of the underworld, for your prize is knowledge and it is only given to the worthy . . . are you ready for your journey of self-discovery?

If so let us begone, let us go back to a magickal time, and who knows, we may well be fortunate enough to be allowed to carry some of this knowledge back. The runes covered in this book are traditionally known as The Elder Futhark Runes. Elder as in being of the oldest set of runes known to us, and Futhark, because of the first six runes in this alphabet. I have used the more commonly used Anglo-Saxon names for the runes as not only were they the names of each rune used in the British Isles, but they are the more common names used in cross-reference with other books.

The Franks Casket

the history of the runes

In times past, our ancestors understood about the cycles of the earth, the moon and the stars. They understood the magick that was contained within such, and used it, worked with it and accepted it as a natural state to be involved with. They lived and worked with this energy and used it to their best advantages.

When our most ancient of ancestors wished to keep a record of things they did so in a pictorial fashion, they used pictures as a written language, so that what they wished to be passed on in a non-aural tradition could be done so with ease.

The establishing of pictures as a historical record and a method of communication is probably best known in ancient Egypt, where the heiroglyphs were used in every circumstance.

Gradually pictures developed into symbols, and eventually into letters, where we have a stage today where letters make words which are not open to negotiation, the word on the page is accepted as being the written word, it has no inner meanings.

But what of pictures! Take the picture of a boat; is it a pleasure boat or a warship, does it carry treasure or the plague. One can only tell by the style of the picture, but what if the picture was a simplistic design like Fig. 1.

FIG. 1

We could not tell by that what the meaning of the boat was, but if we added more pictures around the boat, (FIG. 2) we could tell what was happening in the scene, and as such be able to relay this message in an oral fashion. It was through pictures that the oral tradition transcended into a concept which we have today, which is an interrelated system of both oral and written traditions.

FIG. 2

So it is with runes; each rune is a pictorial symbol, indicative of a particular natural element, and from that element, great things can be learned. Take the rune *IS* (FIG.3).

FIG. 3

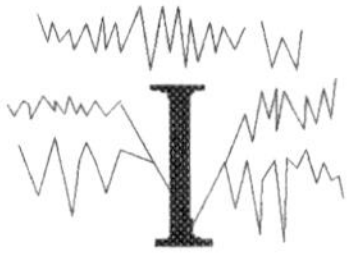

FIG. 4

We can see by FIG. 4 that it is a pictogram of the element of ice, so what can we say of such. Ice hinders, it slows down projects. We could say a lot about ice, we could explain much about the symbolic meaning behind the element of ice, and the symbolic vision it creates.

Runes are magickal alphabets, they are explanations of natural elements that were important to our ancestors. They were used by our ancestors for many magickal purposes, such as the casting of spells, divination, magickal invocation. All skills that were needed within an ancient tribal situation, in a time when the fear of the unknown was very real. In a desperate need for knowing what was coming next, runes took their role as both a guide for divination and as a magickal symbol to invoke a power. Like using Tarot, I Ching, etc., this is a very solemn purpose, and like both Tarot and I Ching, the casting of runes is able to answer specific questions put to the runes and to help to clarify a problem.

According to the ancient Nordic legends the runes were discovered by Odin as he hung for nine days upon Yggdrasil, the world tree, the centre of the Nordic universe. This was seen as a very magickal sacrifice for the benefit of his people, the dead Odin's spirit, descended into the world of the dead, Niflheim, the Underworld.

The Nordic underworld is like the underworld of most other cultures, and the descent into the underworld was seen as a very magickal journey, for it was in the underworld that the soul learned of many things, things that could be taken back to benefit the tribe. It was here in Niflheim, that the spirits of the Old Ones revealed the secrets of the runes to Odin, thus giving him sacred magick. Once he obtained the runes, Odin ascended once again onto the Earth Plane, where he proudly showed his runes to the world.

It was not only in Nordic cultures that runes were used, the Saxons and the Celts both used systems of runic wisdom.

There was a system of runes known to the Celtic Druids, probably a cross-pollination of ideas from Nordic people who did explore the western channel between Wales and Eire. This was an alphabet known as the Coelbran Y Beirdd, or the alphabet of the Bards. There are similarities between these and the Nordic runes. It is in this spirit of self-explanation that we follow the archetype of Odin, and venture into the depths of our own subconscious, to discover for ourselves the power of the runes.

THE HANGED MAN TAROT CARD:

"The essential meaning of this card is one of sacrifice: the voluntary giving up of something in order to get something of greater value. In Teutonic myth, the god Odin volunteered his own sacrifice and rejuvenation. 'For nine nights,' he says in an old poem, 'wounded by my own spear, consecrated to Odin, myself consecrated to myself, I remained hanging from the tree, shaken by the wind, from the mighty tree whose roots men know not.' The tree mentioned was the ash Yggdrasil, the world tree, and by wounding himself and hanging from its branches, Odin performed a magical rite for the purpose of rebirth and rejuvenation. As he hung for those nine lonely days and nights, he waited in vain for someone to bring him food or drink. However, as he hung he looked about carefully at what lay beneath him and noticed some runes - characters carved on stone which have magical meaning and powers. He managed with some considerable effort to pick one up and was immediately released from the tree by their magic. He was filled anew with youth and vigour; and so his resurrection and rejuvenation was accomplished."

The Complete Book of TAROT,
Juliet Sharman-Burke

Obtaining your Runes

Runes for casting have been made out of many materials over the years, from stone, or clay, to wood. All have a particular potency within themselves as they carry within the power of the person who has created them, and that is what is important to remember. Each individual has a power of their own, if you are obtaining your runes from someone else, make sure that you are happy with that for if you are not, then any future use that you will obtain from these runes, you will also question.

If you wish to make your own runes out of whatever material you choose, wood, clay, stone, etc., remember that whilst you are making them you are performing a magickal act, and as such you must concentrate your mind in this direction. Do not let your concentration slip, a good concept is to chant whilst your are making your runes so you are concentrating on the sacred purpose of the runes that you are making — respect from the start is a good concept to have.

If you decide against making your runes and prefer to purchase them you should go for a handmade set rather than plastic or resinous factory made sets. A handmade set has taken a dedicated person time to actually manufacture the runes and so contain a power coming from that person; this power will assist you in your quest for knowledge via the runes. Making runes is a skill and it does take time to make a set properly – in the region of between three and nine hours – please remember this when deciding on rune sets.

Destiny

Most people are under the misunderstanding that methods of divination such as Runes, Tarot, etc., tell you your future! This is not so, methods of divination assert for you the potential of future events so you can be discriminatory towards your interaction with such events.

TAKE NOTE: Your future destiny is not fixed!

It is a series of probabilities and challenges. There is a very good correlation with the concept of Destiny being like a main road and you are driving down it. Along the way you will see a sign post, you have a decision to make, do you accept the turning off the road and go along it, or do you stay on the that road?

How do you know that the road is not a danger and the turning is safety or vice versa? How do you know that the turning off the road could lead you to greater things or greater dangers? How do you know that the turning off the road could lead you to the ultimate disaster, or could that disaster befall you without turning off? You don't!

This is the purpose of the runes; they can give you a natural insight into how the way that things could be in relation to yourself and how things will work out in a personal manner to yourself. Consider the turning in the road, that we shall call life, as being a challenge, a conquest, or a lesson learned. When we have met this challenge, when we have taken our part in a conquest or when we have learned a lesson, we are on our way again. No road comes to a dead end! How do you know that the road that you have taken is but a short cut, a lesson needed and learned, then when you are on your way again you come to another turning off your road, and once again, the same decisions are needed. Do you take the turn off or do you stay on the road? How do you not know that the turn off will lead you back onto the path that you chose to turn off a lesson learned a while ago. Again you don't, but you can accept guidance from your spirit guides that are your runes, for they can give you the insight that you perhaps cannot see.

In this way they are your friends and your guide . . . use them as such, respect them as such; they are magickal tools, each one an age old magickal symbol of power, use them wisely and safely. Do not ridicule the power of these runes, for if you do, then the power that was once yours with them, will be no longer. Divination is not merely to gain a glimpse of the future, nor is it fortune-telling, it is your guide to anticipating future events.

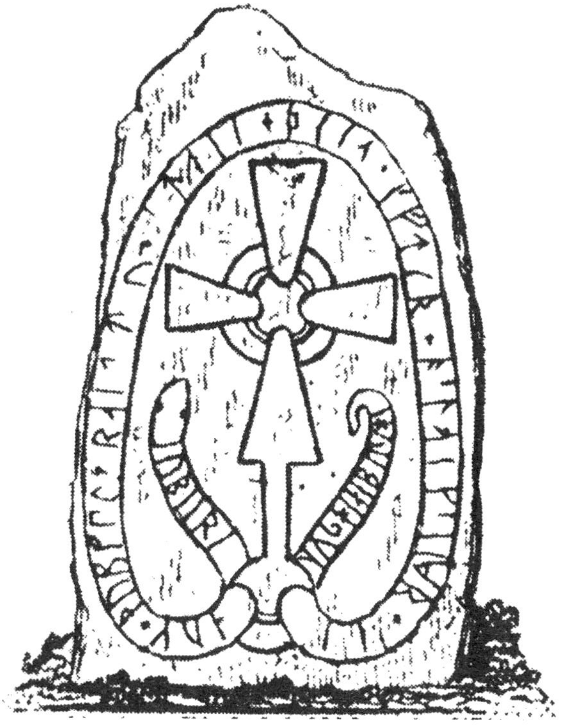

Reading the Runes

For individual purpose there are many ways of reading the runes, each way specifically potent enough to supply you with a very accurate answer. To answer a specific question, i.e., Will I be successful in obtaining a job? Will I be able to help? Is it right for me? etc., a simple magickal act will be sufficient to give an answer. The easiest way to obtain an answer for these purposes is to keep your runes in their bag, and with the question in mind, and your eyes shut, rummage through the bag with your right hand until you feel happy with the rune that you are going to draw.

Take the rune chosen completely out of the bag and examine it, see what message the rune has for you, in the meaning section of this book. From this interpretation you will get a detailed answer which you can interpret as a yes or no, in your quest for an answer to a question that you cannot solve yourself. For a more detailed reading, a more detailed way of reading your runes is needed. For this you will be using all twenty-five runes.

When you place your runes out, you will be placing them in twelve pairs around a circle, with the twenty-fifth rune to be placed in the centre. Your rune circle should look like the diagram opposite:–

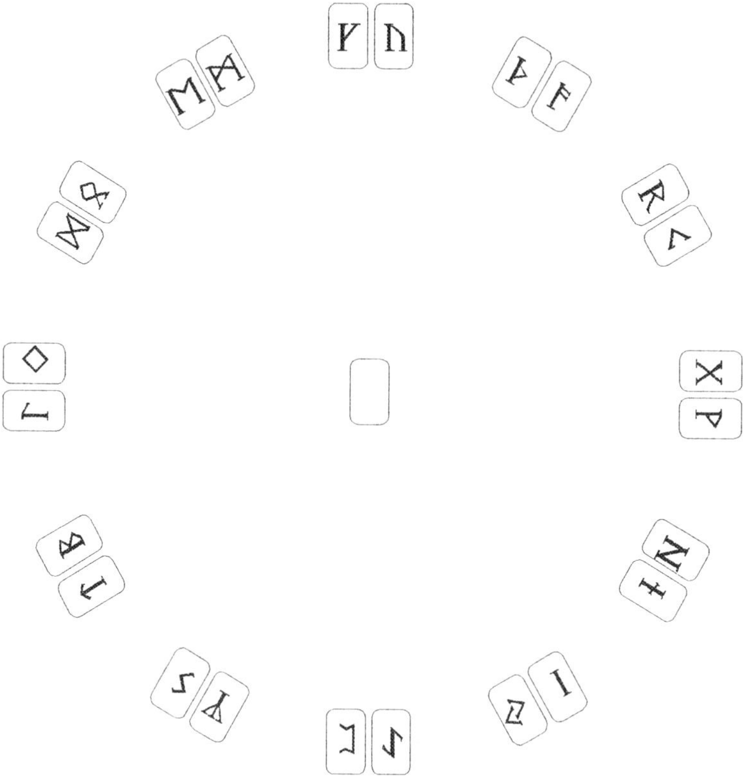

RUNE CIRCLE

Each of the specific houses of the circle have a particular meaning, and starting from the west is where you should place your first pair of runes. The circle of houses go in a Widdershins direction that relates to the astrological correspondences of the houses. The houses for the reading should be as laid out below.

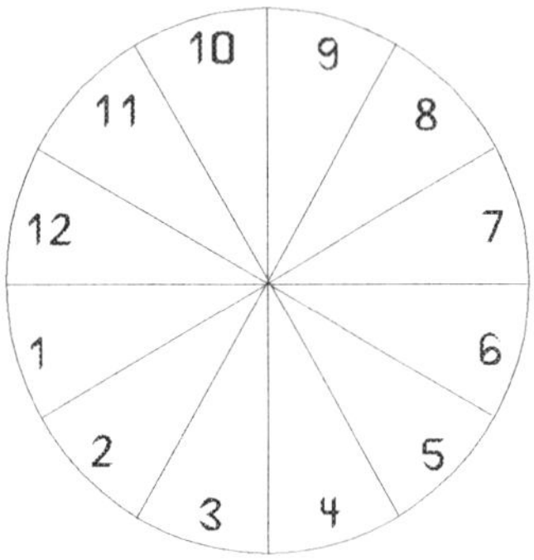

The meaning of the individual houses are :-

House	Meaning
1	The situation, that is the person's situation who is asking the advice of the runes. It is you in the role of rune master, seeking advice, and the state of mind, and state of energy, as to the person asking the advice. If the reading is for a third party then the first house represents their situation and not the readers.
2	Matters concerning money or financial situations, answers given by the runes direct towards this aspect of a problem.
3	Communications, media, telephone, etc., are all covered within the third house. Answers to the negative generally indicate a lack of communication as being the problem.
4	The family, home environment or immediate surroundings concerning the querent.

House	Meaning
5	The hopes and fears of the querent are manifested through this house. It is a house of chance or things that are not cut and dry, or definite.
6	Health and personal problems are shown through this house. If very negative answers are given through this house, do not consider them to be bad omens, but rather manifestations of warnings about impending ill health, and should be considered as such.
7	As the first house is how the reader deals with a situation, this house deals with how people associated with the reader on a personal level, maybe a sexual partner, can accept the forthcoming situation.
8	Inheritance, financial gifts and other unforeseen are covered within the eighth house.
9	The dreams or desires of the querent are controlled with this house. It represents the material desires rather than the spiritual needs.
10	The house of career and work, and the forthcoming events that will affect it. It affects all the other houses, and acts as a balance. It is the establishment of the rest of the reading and how it reflects with this house.
11	This is the spiritual house for the querent, it indicates the things that are of importance to the querent on a spiritual level and how they will be affected by the rest of the reading. A house of warning and attention, to be studied extremely carefully as it bears a reflection through the rest of the houses.
12	The negative aspects of the querent. It shows personal flaws in the person and manifestations of such, such as laziness, greed, anger, resentment, jealousy, hate, etc.

To place the runes, draw them from their pouch two-at-a-time, again concentrating upon the purpose of each of the houses. Place them in their pairs at each of the houses, going round the circle in an anticlockwise (or Widdershins) direction, placing two at each of the points of the circle.

You will have one rune left over, this is the rune of Destiny or 'Wyrd Rune'. This is the uncontrollable fate of the reader, the rest of the runes bear relevance to their particular houses, this rune bears a relevance to the whole reading. You can then proceed to instigate the reading, starting at the first house and systematically working your way round them.

There are many methods of reading the runes, these are just two of them. They are sufficient for a beginner to know and get to know about the runes and the way in which they bear relevance to each other.

You can devise your own way of reading the runes, this is perfectly acceptable, as you will be enhancing the power of the runes with your own magickal power, and will be using them in a way that is very personal to you. It will be your own form of power reading, that is solely yours and for you to understand.

If you do get to devise your own rune spreads, please remember that you will have to take into account the power of the Wyrd Rune, the power of destiny, so make provision for this in your readings.

the meanings of the runes

Each rune was allocated to a different aspect of daily life, and the importance that that aspect held for the benefit of the tribe in an interrelated family situation. The problem of one person was the problem of all. These everyday mundane situations, and their more spiritual and deeper aspects, had to be taken into consideration when problem solving, as there is not only two sides to a coin — but the edge as well.

The magick of the runes and their influence upon the natural world represented to our ancestors the answers to all universal questions contained within one universal space. The runes as magickal tools of divination were important, each one of the runes has their own symbolic meaning, the pouch in which the runes were contained was the essence of the earth and all things contained within it, the ground or cloth upon which the runes were cast was the personal situation of the querent — each one was interrelated and important to each other.

The runes were associated to three families or Aettir. The word Eight being a derivation of the Nordic word Aett, which indicated the eight magickal directions. Freya, Hagal and Tyr being the guardian deities over each respective Aett, with each Aett bearing a relevance to the runes contained within such.

Deity	Aett
Freya	ᚠ ᚢ ᚦ ᚨ ᚱ ᚲ ᚷ ᚹ Feoh Ur Thorn As Rad Ken Gyfu Wyn The runes of Freya's Aett concern matters of love, achievement and creative energies. It is the reflection of these runes upon the others that give clarity to the immediate problem to be encountered.

Deity	Aett
Hagal	ᚺ ᚾ ᛁ ᛃ ᛇ ᛈ ᛉ ᛊ Hagal Nyd Is Jera Eoh Peorth Elhaz Sigil The runes of Hagal's Aett are the runes of achievement, opportunity and success. It is also the Aett of karma, and will assert whether something is right or wrong. Regarding rune magick, it will give an indication of the validity of a solution to a problem.
Tyr	ᛏ ᛒ ᛖ ᛗ ᛚ ᛜ ᛟ ᛞ Tyr Beorc Ehwaz Man Lagu Ing Odal Daeg These are the runes of spiritual attainment and mental achievement. Their reflection upon a situation is highlighted upon their reflection upon runes of the other two Aettir. These runes determine the correct outcome of the situation.

Interpretation of Individual Runes

ᚠ

FEOH

Interpretation :-
To our ancient ancestors, the acquisition of cattle was an indication of wealth. This rune indicates a wealth but a wealth that must be worked for, not one that will come easily. It is something that is desirous to be obtained, and something that will be cared for. It could also indicate help which will be respected, or a love that has to be obtained from another person.

Deity:	**Freya**	Element:	**Fire**
Polarity:	**Female**	Solar time cycle:	**03:00 29 June 08:00 14 July**
Common letter:	**F**		
Numerological value:	**1**	Esoteric symbol:	**The Primal Earth Mother**
Colour value:	**Brown**		
Magickal sound:	**ffff (Soft)**	Other names:	**Feo, F, Fehu, Frew, Feh**
Ancient meaning:	**Cattle**		
Tree:	**Elder**	Keyword:	**Acquisition**
Herb:	**Nettle**		

Anglo-Saxon Casket with runic inscription

Interpretation of Individual Runes

ᚢ

UR

Interpretation :-
The Wild Oxen was not only a prize but an omen of change, often sudden and dramatic, which needs to be adapted to. Indicates also a challenge which has to be confronted. It is the manifestation of physical strength that is needed to overcome the obstacle which is to be encountered.

Deity:	**Thor**	Element:	**Earth**
Polarity:	**Male**	Solar time cycle:	**08:00 14 July 13:59 29 July**
Common letter:	**U**		
Numerological value:	**2**	Esoteric symbol:	**The Horns of the Wild Oxen**
Colour value:	**Green**		
Magickal sound:	**uuuuuh (Soft)**	Other names:	**Ur, Uur, Uraz, Uruz, Urus**
Ancient meaning:	**Wild Oxen**		
Tree:	**Birch**	Keyword:	**Confrontation**
Herb:	**Iceland Moss**		

ᚦ

THORN

Interpretation :- The elemental forces contained within nature manifest themselves within the rune Thorn. It is an indication of protection. As protection of the person involved is at stake, it could also be seen as a rune of incitement or attack, but be warned, if used for this end, then the threefold law of return will take its course. Attack can also be against yourself, so take this as a warning within a reading, that someone is about to attack.

Deity:	**Thor**	Element:	**Fire**
Polarity:	**Male**	Solar time cycle:	**14:00 29 July 18:59 13 Aug.**
Common letter:	**Th**		
Numerological value:	**3**	Esoteric symbol:	**The Hammer of Thor**
Colour value:	**White**		
Magickal sound:	**tttthhhh (Hard)**	Other names:	**Thurs, Thursiaz, Thor, Thursis, Thyth**
Ancient meaning:	**Ice Demon**		
Tree:	**Thorn/Oak**		
Herb:	**House Leek**	Keyword:	**Challenge**

Interpretation of Individual Runes

ᚨ

AS

Interpretation :-
As Odin is the Lord of the Runes, so this is the rune of his honour. It is the symbol of the quest for truth and wisdom. The Shamanic Sigil of quest or knowledgeable challenge. This is the runic invocation of power.

Deity:	**Odin**	Element:	**Air**
Polarity:	**Male**	Solar time cycle:	**19:00 13 Aug. 00:00 29 Aug.**
Common letter:	**A/O**		
Numerological value:	**4**	Esoteric symbol:	**The World Tree**
Colour value:	**Purple**		
Magickal sound:	**aaaaah (Hard)**	Other names:	**Os, Asa, Ansuz, Ansus, Aza, Aesc**
Ancient meaning:	**A God or deity**		
Tree:	**Ash**		
Herb:	**Amanita Muscaria**	Keyword:	**Knowledge**

ᚱ

RADH

Interpretation :- The possibility of travel, matters concerning transport or journeys, or the arrival of unexpected news. This is the symbol of fertility, and a good luck symbol for the prospects of a project to be good. It could therefore be seen as a unifying symbol of good news, transport and wealth — a good time for business trips. Also a good time for making future plans or planning a long-term project.

Deity:	**Tyr**	Element:	**Air**
Polarity:	**Male**	Solar time cycle:	**00:00 29 Aug. 06:00 13 Sept.**
Common letter:	**R**		
Numerological value:	**5**	Esoteric symbol:	**The Wheel of the Cart**
Colour value:	**Black**		
Magickal sound:	**hrrrrrh (Soft)**	Other names:	**Rd, Reid, Rait, Raiso, Raidha**
Ancient meaning:	**Chariot**		
Tree:	**Oak**	Keyword:	**Journeying**
Herb:	**Mugwort**		

ᚲ

KEN

Interpretation :-
The shining light of a creative force. Light was very important to our ancestors, it was a particular need, as with fire and light came warmth. This is a time when all special projects can benefit from new light being shed upon them, or time to learn something new, as everything seen in a new light is enlightening.

Deity:	**Frey**	Element:	**Fire**
Polarity:	**Female**	Solar time cycle:	**06:00 13 Sept.** **11:00 28 Sept.**
Common letter:	**K**		
Numerological value:	**6**	Esoteric symbol:	**Sacred Fire**
Colour value:	**Yellow**		
Magickal sound:	**kkkka (Hard)**	Other names:	**Kaan, Cen, Kenaz, Chaon**
Ancient meaning:	**Torch, Light**		
Tree:	**Pine**	Keyword:	**Enlightenment**
Herb:	**Cowslip**		

X

GYFU

Interpretation :-
Hospitality and generosity was an important aspect to life. It was through the generosity of others that people were able to survive when times became hard. This is a rune of charity, tolerance and giving. A gift may be a physical gift, or it might be the gift of caring for someone. It could also be the gift of new love or even a birth.

Deity:	**Odin**	Element:	**Air**
Polarity:	**Male & Female**	Solar time cycle:	**11:00 28 Sept.** **16:00 13 Oct.**
Common letter:	**G**		
Numerological value:	**7**	Esoteric symbol:	**Sacred Marking**
Colour value:	**Red**		
Magickal sound:	**guh (Hard)**	Other names:	**Gibo, Gebo, Giba, Gewa**
Ancient meaning:	**A Gift**		
Tree:	**Elm**	Keyword:	**Receiving**
Herb:	**Hearts ease**		

Interpretation of Individual Runes

ᚹ

WYNN

Interpretation :-
This is the rune of ultimate achievement. It is an aspect of the feeling that one gets when you are in a happy or joyous state, the feeling that all is well with the world, you feel peace and contentment, a happy outcome to any problem.

Deity:	**Odin**	Element:	**Earth**
Polarity:	**Male**	Solar time cycle:	**16:00 13 Oct. 22:00 28 Oct**
Common letter:	**W**		
Numerological value:	**8**	Esoteric symbol:	**Flag**
Colour value:	**Blue**		
Magickal sound:	**ooouuuuh (Soft)**	Other names:	**Wunna, Winja, Wunjo, Winne, Wunnaz**
Ancient meaning:	**Joyous / Perfection**		
Tree:	**Ash**	Keyword:	**Contentment**
Herb:	**Flax**		

ᚺ

HAGAL

Interpretation :-
The forces at work around you are beyond your control, they have to be accepted, regardless of the outcome. This could indicate a setback in any plans that you may be putting into action at present. It is far better to wait until this time passes, rather than expend wasteful energy on trying to fight it.

Deity:	**Heimdall**	Element:	**Water**
Polarity:	**Female**	Solar time cycle:	**22:00 28 Oct. 03:00 13 Nov.**
Common letter:	**H**		
Numerological value:	**1**	Esoteric symbol:	**The Serpent**
Colour value:	**White**		
Magickal sound:	**hhhhhuh (Soft)**	Other names:	**Hagal, Hagalaz, Hgalaz, Hagl**
Ancient meaning:	**Hail / Frost**		
Tree:	**Yew**	Keyword:	**Chaos**
Herb:	**Briony**		

NYD

Interpretation :-
A wanting and a time of need. The main lesson to be learned with this rune is, of course, patience. The way in which you anticipate that things will work out may not be to your liking, therefore, the need in this is patience. Nyd is both a stumbling block, for you to come unstuck and a power. The magick lies in what you anticipate to be your Need!

Deity:	**Frigga**	Element:	**Fire**
Polarity:	**Female**	Solar time cycle:	**03:00 13 Nov. 08:00 28 Nov.**
Common letter:	**N**		
Numerological value:	**2**	Esoteric symbol:	**Fire Bow and Block**
Colour value:	**Blue**		
Magickal sound:	**nnnnn (Hard)**	Other names:	**Need, Nid, Noicz, Naudhiz, Nauthiz, Naudh**
Ancient meaning:	**Need**		
Tree:	**Beech**		
Herb:	**Snakeroot**	Keyword:	**Desire**

IS

Interpretation :-
Stagnation of ideas and plans that are in mind need to be held over for a more fortunate time. This wait could also be what is needed for you to think the plans out fully before executing them. This is a period of cooling down any emotive ideas that you may have need to be controlled, it is a good rune to do this.

Deity:	**Skadi**	Element:	**Water**
Polarity:	**Female**	Solar time cycle:	**08:00 28 Nov. 14:00 13 Dec.**
Common letter:	**I**		
Numerological value:	**3**	Esoteric symbol:	**Sacred Ice**
Colour value:	**Black**		
Magickal sound:	**yyyyy (Hard)**	Other names:	**Iss, Isa, Eis, Iiz**
Ancient meaning:	**Ice**		
Tree:	**Alder**	Keyword:	**Isolation**
Herb:	**Henbane**		

JERA

Interpretation :-
This is very important, this is the manifestation of hard work put into a project and now you can see the fruits of your labours by the results which you are achieving. As you have sown, so you will reap! This is a time of prosperity and of fruitful labours, a time of relaxation for it indicates that plans put into action will succeed.

Deity:	**Frey/Freya**	Element:	**Earth**
Polarity:	**Male / Female**	Solar time cycle:	**14:00 13 Dec. 19:00 28 Dec.**
Common letter:	**Y**		
Numerological value:	**4**	Esoteric symbol:	**Sacred Marriage**
Colour value:	**Brown**		
Magickal sound:	**jjjjuh (Hard)**	Other names:	**Yar, Jara, Jer, Ger, Ar**
Ancient meaning:	**Harvest**		
Tree:	**Oak**	Keyword:	**Fruitfulness**
Herb:	**Rosemary**		

EOH

Interpretation :-
The symbol of unification, the central pillar of the pulling together of all energies to combine into a greater force, thus magickally instilling each of the elements. The symbol of the perfect foundation of a project or plan. As the Yew is a tree of protection so is this rune, it indicates the warding off of a problem, the protection of a person against a problem.

Deity:	**Odin**	Element:	**Earth**
Polarity:	**Male**	Solar time cycle:	**19:00 28 Dec. 01:00 13 Jan.**
Common letter:	**E / I**		
Numerological value:	**5**	Esoteric symbol:	**The Trunk of the Yew Tree**
Colour value:	**Green**		
Magickal sound:	**ih (Hard)**	Other names:	**Eo, Eihwaz, Eys, Ihwar**
Ancient meaning:	**Yew Tree**		
Tree:	**Yew**	Keyword:	**Togetherness**
Herb:	**Briony**		

Interpretation of Individual Runes

ᛈ PEORTH

Interpretation :-
The meaning of the Peorth or Per rune has never been interpreted, it indicates a hidden mystery, or revelation in that something hidden will come to light. This could be as mundane as finding a lost object, or the revelation of the answer to a question. This indicates a good time for concentrating on matters spiritual, as you will be working with the hidden forces in your favour.

Deity:	**Frigg**	Element:	**Water**
Polarity:	**Female**	Solar time cycle:	**01:00 13 Jan. 05:00 28 Jan.**
Common letter:	**P**		
Numerological value:	**6**	Esoteric symbol:	**The Womb**
Colour value:	**Red**		
Magickal sound:	**peh (Hard)**	Other names:	**Purt, Perthro, Pertra, Paithra**
Ancient meaning:	**Unknown**		
Tree:	**Beech**	Keyword:	**Mystery**
Herb:	**Aconite**		

ᛉ ELHAZ

Interpretation :- This is a rune of good fortune and unexpected good luck. The Elhaz rune is the symbol of protection for the person, and is a symbol of life. It is reputed to be of great use in warding off the evil-eye. The Nordic people attribute Elhaz to the Elk, which was both hunted and protected in its natural state to encourage future use of the Elk both for meat, skin, bone, etc. To protect and be protected — a good indication.

Deity:	**Heimdall**	Element:	**Air**
Polarity:	**Male/Female**	Solar time cycle:	**05:00 28 Jan. 10:00 12 Feb.**
Common letter:	**Z**		
Numerological value:	**7**	Esoteric symbol:	**The Elk**
Colour value:	**Purple**		
Magickal sound:	**sz (Hard)**	Other names:	**Akiz, Eolh, Eolx, Algiz, Algia**
Ancient meaning:	**Protection**		
Tree:	**Yew**		
Herb:	**Sedge**	Keyword:	**Defence**

ᛊ SIGIL

Interpretation :-
The essential power and vitality that is needed in the creation of all things. This rune indicates the truth of how things will be. It is a rune of victory and success. It is the rune of triumph of light over dark, good over evil.

Deity:	**Balder**	Element:	**Air**
Polarity:	**Male**	Solar time cycle:	**10:00 12 Feb. 16:00 27 Feb.**
Common letter:	**S**		
Numerological value:	**8**	Esoteric symbol:	**The Sacred Sun**
Colour value:	**Yellow**		
Magickal sound:	**sss (Soft)**	Other names:	**Sigel, Sig, Sigi, Sowulo**
Ancient meaning:	**The Sun**		
Tree:	**Juniper**	Keyword:	**Enthusiasm**
Herb:	**Mistletoe**		

ᛏ TYR

Interpretation :-
This is a rune of motivation, the desire to win. It is a rune of success in whatever battle or conflict that one is placed within. It is an indication of victory, especially within a repressed situation such as in legal matters.

Deity:	**Tyr**	Element:	**Air**
Polarity:	**Male**	Solar time cycle:	**16:00 27 Feb. 21:00 14 Mar.**
Common letter:	**T**		
Numerological value:	**1**	Esoteric symbol:	**The Heavens**
Colour value:	**Red**		
Magickal sound:	**tuh (Hard)**	Other names:	**Tiw, Teiwaz, Tiews, Tir, Tyz**
Ancient meaning:	**The God Tyr**		
Tree:	**Oak**	Keyword:	**Zest**
Herb:	**Sage**		

Interpretation of Individual Runes

ᛒ

BEORC

Interpretation :-
A rune of healing and recovery, an indication of regeneration and renewal. It is the rebirth of projects or plans. Any plans already in action, and are under this rune, will need nurturing and caring for until they are able to look after themselves. The Beorc rune is also indicative of children and matters concerning children.

Deity:	**Holda**	Element:	**Earth**
Polarity:	**Female**	Solar time cycle:	**21:00 14 March 02:00 30 March**
Common letter:	**B**		
Numerological value:	**2**	Esoteric symbol:	**The Breasts of the Earth**
Colour value:	**Blue**		
Magickal sound:	**behh (Soft)**	Other names:	**Berkana, Bercna, Brica, Bjarkan, Borg**
Ancient meaning:	**Birch Tree**		
Tree:	**Birch**		
Herb:	**Ladies Mantle**	Keyword:	**Self-regeneration**

ᛖ

EHWAZ

Interpretation :- The indication of travel by land is well aspected. The moving aspect of Ehwaz may also mean that a moving of house, a change of job, or a change in domestic circumstances is well looked after. There is a dual aspect to Ehwaz, and some rune masters consider that Ehwaz is in fact a pair of horses and if this is accepted, then the duality of protector and protection is also brought into play.

Deity:	**Frey/Freya**	Element:	**Earth**
Polarity:	**Male/Female**	Solar time cycle:	**02:00 30 March 07:00 14 April**
Common letter:	**E**		
Numerological value:	**3**	Esoteric symbol:	**The Mother Goddess**
Colour value:	**White**		
Magickal sound:	**ehhh (Soft)**	Other names:	**Eko, Eh, Eoh, Aihws**
Ancient meaning:	**Horses**		
Tree:	**Oak**	Keyword:	**Adventure**
Herb:	**Ragwort**		

ᛗ MANN

Interpretation :-
The need for others around you, the protection of a tribal society, your family, indicating that this is not a time to go it alone, seek advice and assistance from others. It could also show a distrust from other men, and an indication that deception is possible.

Deity:	**Odin**	Element:	**Air**
Polarity:	**Male / Female**	Solar time cycle:	**07:00 14 April 12:00 29 April**
Common letter:	**M**		
Numerological value:	**4**	Esoteric symbol:	**The Union of Heaven & Earth**
Colour value:	**Purple**		
Magickal sound:	**mmaah (Soft)**	Other names:	**Maan, Mannaz, Manna, Madur Madhr**
Ancient meaning:	**Man**		
Tree:	**Holly**		
Herb:	**Madder**	Keyword:	**Mankind**

ᛚ LAGU

Interpretation :- A rune with dual meanings, some give the concept of a lake, as being travel over water, others as a rune of healing, as the leek is, a neutraliser of poison. I think the main purpose of this rune is an indication for you to follow your own intuition and consider what is wrong or right in your own opinions, rather than listening to what others have to say to you. Follow your own psychic instinct and you will not go far wrong.

Deity:	**Njord**	Element:	**Water**
Polarity:	**Female**	Solar time cycle:	**12:00 29 April 18:00 14 May**
Common letter:	**L**		
Numerological value:	**5**	Esoteric symbol:	**Sea Wave**
Colour value:	**Green**		
Magickal sound:	**lllll (Soft)**	Other names:	**Laukiz, Laguz, Laughar, Logr, Lago**
Ancient meaning:	**Lake or leek**		
Tree:	**Osier**		
Herb:	**Leek**	Keyword:	**Decide**

Interpretation of Individual Runes

ING

Interpretation :-
Often associated with the god Freya. This is a rune of fruition, a fertile conclusion of any plan that you may have in mind. It is a good indication of future success. This rune could also be the ease of worry from any stressful situations that a person is under.

Deity:	**Ing**	Element:	**Earth**
Polarity:	**Male/Female**	Solar time cycle:	**18:00 14 May 23:00 29 May**
Common letter:	**Ng**		
Numerological value:	**6**	Esoteric symbol:	**The genitals**
Colour value:	**Black**		
Magickal sound:	**ng (Hard)**	Other names:	**Ingwaz, Inguz, Enguz, Iggws, Ine, Yngvi**
Ancient meaning:	**A fertility god**		
Tree:	**Apple**		
Herb:	**Chamomile**	Keyword:	**Creative achievement**

ODAL

Interpretation :-
Concerning matters of property and other inheritances. It is a rune of both wealth and prosperity, and of responsibility for all that which is in your trust. You have not acquired things for your self but are merely holding it in trust for your children — like mankind is for the earth, we all have a responsibility for our children!

Deity:	**Odin**	Element:	**Earth**
Polarity:	**Male**	Solar time cycle:	**23:00 29 May 04:00 14 June**
Common letter:	**O**		
Numerological value:	**7**	Esoteric symbol:	**The Earth**
Colour value:	**Brown**		
Magickal sound:	**oh (Soft)**	Other names:	**Ethel, Aethel, Odil, Oldhal, Othala, Utal**
Ancient meaning:	**The homestead**		
Tree:	**Hawthorn**		
Herb:	**Clover**	Keyword:	**Security**

ᛞ

DAEG

Interpretation :- The here and now of a situation, the steady progression of things. Acknowledgement that things are as they should be and are progressing slowly. This is a rune of immediate attitude, a time when things must be done immediately whilst you are working with the correct current. This is a rune of stimulation, of promoting growth within a situation and of empowering it with the energy of the Day.

Deity:	**Heimdall**	Element:	**Fire**
Polarity:	**Male**	Solar time cycle:	**04:00 14 June 03:00 29 June**
Common letter:	**D**		
Numerological value:	**8**	Esoteric symbol:	**Balance of the Day and Night**
Colour value:	**Yellow**		
Magickal sound:	**ddae (Soft)**	Other names:	**Dagaz, Dags, Dagr, Daaz, Tag**
Ancient meaning:	**Day**		
Tree:	**Spruce**	Keyword:	**Concernment**
Herb:	**Clary sage**		

WYRD

Interpretation :-

Along with the three families of runes there is the blank twenty-fifth rune, the WYRD Rune. This indicates the role of destiny in all of the runes, it guides through all of the above runes and governs their position. It is the magickal rune within the set and should not be kept separate from the others in the pouch. It is its interaction with the other runes that creates a magickal environment for the rest of the runes to work.

the Language of the Runes

In the runic language, the word Aett means eight. It is said as it is spelled. In the runic language of our ancestors, in an age before correct grammatical dogma, the vagaries of the English language was not in evidence, each of the runes intoned a particular sound, that was manifest through the rune itself.

It was a rune of power, it was a sound of power. It was the sound itself, put together with other runic sounds that were used to create words, in the same way that our letters are put together to make words. But, in the era before spelling and grammar, it was in the way that a word was put together that mattered not how it was spelt, for it was in the way that it was assembled that its magick was contained within. Spelling was down to the individual, therefore we have different spellings of the names of the runes, all are correct, for what they are doing is reflecting the energy of that rune and by giving it a name, it could be identified in oral conversation.

It is possible to use the words in a magickal sense, to translate them into the English Language, or any other language for that matter, as a form of identifying with them for magickal purposes, as in a language that you are familiar with and use, you will be using the runes to link them into your subconscious and to attach a magickal meaning to that particular word.

Look at the word POWER itself — it comprises of the runes :-

ᛈ	ᛟ	ᚹ	ᛇ	ᚱ
Peorth	Odal	Wynn	Eoh	Rad

The word has been translated from a written point of view into its five composite parts.

What about the word THANK. It comprises of the runes:-

ᚦ	ᛁ	ᛜ	ᚲ
Thorn	Is	Ing	Ken

As you can see, two of the 'English' letters have been combined in 'Th', as in the runes, it is not complimentary letter association that we after on a one-to-one basis, but rather a numerological equivalent of sound values. Use this guide when translating words from actual quality to runic quality, and note also how the value changes numerologically!

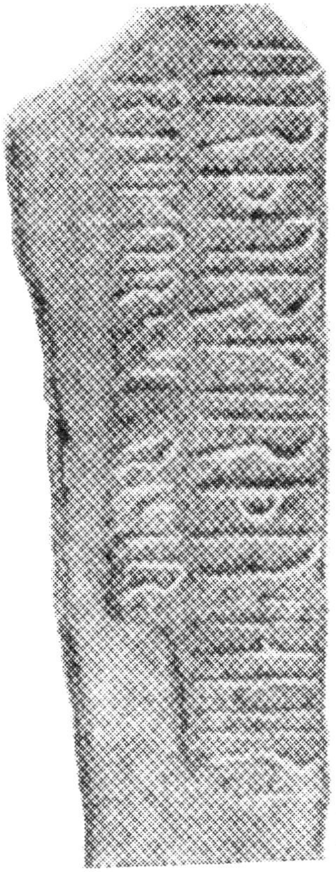

Rune magick

In the natural world of magick, there are many symbols and signs of power. They are natural elements that we can harness in creating a magick of our own, for what we are doing is enhancing the very power that we all possess, with natural symbols of power.

Runes are such symbols of power!

Runes contain power for they, in their smallest form, often as little as but one line, depict a natural power or source of power that mankind can learn and benefit from, when used within magick. The power that runes contain can be put to use in many magickal ways. They can be used as a divination aid, as a power to invoke or banish, as a power to link the subconscious psyche into a greater energy force, that of the different components of the natural world. All this and more is possible through a simple symbol.

With creative magick, the power of the runes have an important use, within a magickal context, that of being able to invoke and direct power through themselves. As a symbol, the rune is a very potent conjurer of power, through being a description within a symbol of the natural manifestation of power that each symbol, symbolically represents its meaning and its relative and associate magickal values.

Runic Meditations

It is very easy to meditate upon a symbol and to fill oneself with the energy of that symbol, thus empowering ones self with the symbolic quality and value of that rune. To do this, it is best to redraw the rune, keeping the artistic quality of a perfect rune very much to the fore, as to meditate upon a symbol that you are not happy with, is a great stumbling block to start with. You should draw the rune to be used, with its correct balance, etc., onto a card approximately A4 (10 x 7) size. It is particularly powerful if you draw the rune in black upon the colour card that is significant to the particular rune. (Colour correspondences of each individual rune given in the section *The Meaning of the Runes.*)

This can be done within a temple, grove, etc., or if you wish to give yourself some sacred space, you can cast a circle if you so desire, (see my book *Wicca Awakens* for details of how to do this) or, alternatively, you can perform this exercise outdoors, thus invoking the sacredness of the natural spirit. If you wish to create atmosphere, you can burn incense, play some gentle music, etc., to get you into a relaxed state.

The card with the rune upon it should stand in front of you, so you can see it when you are either sitting, squatting or standing comfortably. Without staring, look at the rune upon the card in a comfortable and relaxed manner, start a continuous breathing exercise so you are conscious of your breathing. Pull the image of the rune off the card and project towards you (this is a technique of creative visualisation, again see Wicca Awakens for details of this technique).

You can see the image of the rune approximately four inches from your face, you can feel the power coming from it, you can feel it burning your face. Feel the power from it, feel the force that it is emanating, remember this as being the particular power of this symbol. Now let your concentrative force again take the rune from near your face and deposit it back on the card.

Relax and take time to come round from this exercise. If a circle has been cast, banish it. Make a note of everything that you have felt, any visual images conjured up, any visions or insight, make a note of this in your magickal record.

Stone Cross
Lancaster

talismanic magick

It is possible to use the runes as a form of talismanic magick to create a talisman for a unique and individual need. To do this is quite simple but effective procedure. Determine the result required from your talisman (consult the tables in *Planet Magick* or *A Witches Kitchen* for this purpose). Using the correspondences from either book, devise what colour orientation you will be using, what colour paper and pen you will use, what colour candles, what incense to be used, etc. Prepare all of your equipment together, if you feel the need of casting a circle do so (and for the beginner this as a an essential for all magickal work).

Design the talisman beforehand as to how you wish it to look and with the correct influences put into it. Draw the talisman, using the runes, symbols, etc., that you require. Consecrate that talisman as to that particular purpose and close the circle down. Below, I have drawn a talisman for my own particular purpose — this gives some idea of design, etc.

Runes as a magickal alphabet

Runes, after all, were the written language of the Nordic people, their power and energy coming through as a symbol for a greater whole, they are the essential microcosm of a macrocosm, a lesser indicating and carrying within it the same power as the greater. It is, therefore, quite in keeping with runic tradition, to use the runes as an alphabet of power when naming magickal objects, tools, etc. Our pagan ancestors used runes in naming ceremonies, therefore so should we, as in doing so we are carrying on a greater tradition.

There are many legends of fabled swords called 'Dragon Slayer'; 'Defender of Maidens'; 'Champion of the People' — they were all named and empowered with a runic inscription to give them the runic power that their name suggests. Use this as a guideline when naming your own tools, create your own names, bearing in mind the purpose that you will be using the tool for. There is very little us in calling your wand 'Death Head' if you are using it for healing!

The Franks Casket

Bind-Runes

A bind-rune is several runes bound together to give a single magickal symbol of power — a key to unlock greater powers contained within the individual runes, but with them combined with other runes of power, the power of each symbol is infinitely enhanced. Bind-runes are special runes, they are runes of purpose, each bind-rune has been designed for a particular purpose in mind within a magickal context.

It was the shamans and wise ones of Old who combined several runes into a singular magickal Sigil that had this sole purpose. Often these bind-runes were for protection, protection for the home, protection in battle, protection in childbirth, wherever there was a need for protection or for attack even, to attack demons that stalked in the night, there was bind-runes to combat this danger. You can create your own bind-runes for your own particular purposes, as a singular magickal Sigil of power. Remember though, when you are creating bind-runes, that the runes illustrated in this book with their particular meanings are in a perfect balance, they are the correct way round. To invert runes is to negate their meanings therefore the Rune Elhaz, when shown as a protector is standing erect, thus. To negate it and create a rune of attack invert it thus.

Erect Elhaz

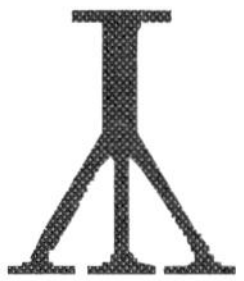

Inverted Elhaz

Following are some bind-runes that I have created for particular circumstances, please gain inspiration from them, note their form and elegance in creating your own bind-runes.

For protection
whilst horse riding

For protection
of the home

To gain justice

To heal a child

To gain inspiration

For protection
in the night

It may well seem to be entertaining creating bind-runes, but please never forget the seriousness of that which is fun. Runes are powerful, combined into bind-runes they are especially powerful!

The Futharks

Germanic Futhark

Used mainly in Scandinavia approx. A.D. 200 – A.D. 700.

Younger (Normal) Futhark

Used mainly in Denmark from around A.D. 800.

Younger (Short Twig) Futhark

Used mainly in Norway-Sweden from around A.D. 800.

Staveless (Haslinge) Runes

Swedish origin, around ten inscriptions, found in Halsingland, Medelpad, Uppland and Sodermanland. A shorthand form for carving on wood. Phonetic values are decided by the number, position and direction of the secondary staffs.

The Medieval Futhark

A later alpahabet developed to correspond to Latin.

The germanic Futhark

ᚠ	ᚢ	ᚦ	ᚨ	ᚱ	ᚲ
f	u	þ	ā	r	k
ᚷ	ᚹ	ᚺ	ᚾ	ᛁ	ᛃ
g	w	h	n	i	j
ᛇ	ᛈ	ᛉ	ᛊ	ᛏ	ᛒ
œ	p	R	s	t	b
ᛖ	ᛗ	ᛚ	ᛜ	ᛞ	ᛟ
e	m	l	rg	d	o

The Younger (normal) Futhark

ᚠ	ᚢ	ᚦ	ᚭ	ᚱ	ᚴ
f	i	þ	ą	r	k
ᚼ	ᚾ	ᛁ	ᛅ	ᛋ	ᛏ
h	n	i	a	s	t
ᛒ	ᛘ	ᛚ	ᛦ		
b	m	l	R		

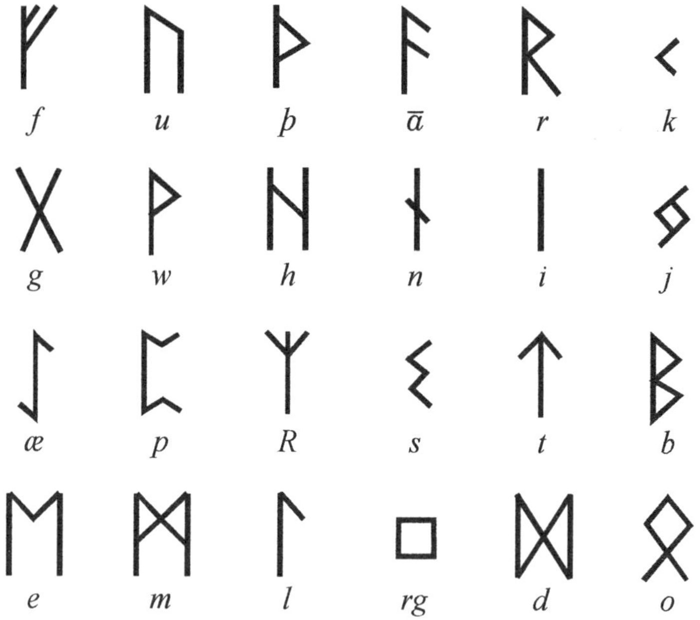

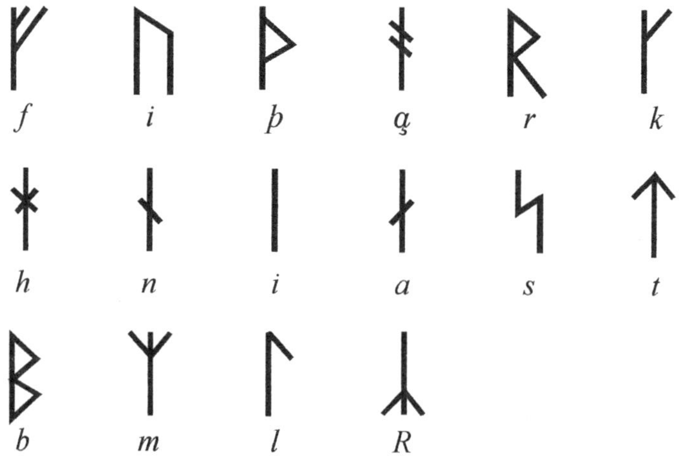

The Younger (short twig) Futhark

f	u	þ	ą	r	k
h	n	i	a	s	t
b	m	l	R		

Staveless (hälsinge) Runes

f	i	þ	ą	r	k
h	n	i	a	s	t
b	m	l	R		

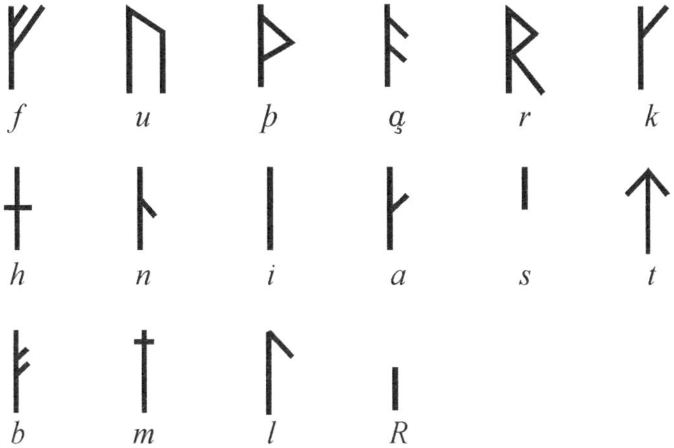

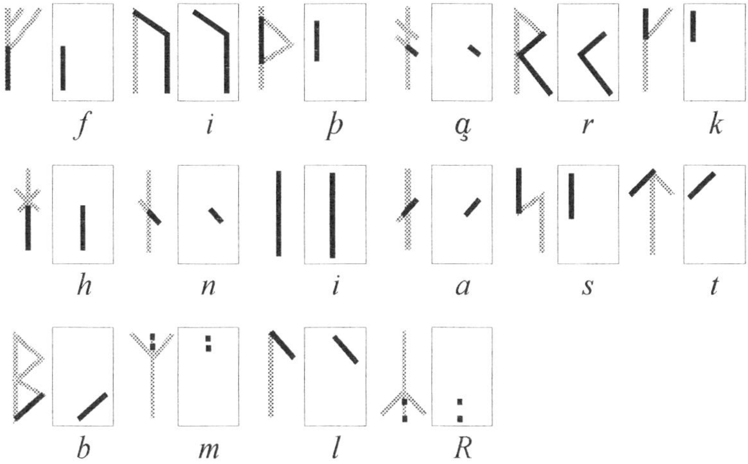

The Medieval Futhark

a	b	c	d	þ	ð
e	f	g	h	i	k
l	m	n	o	p	q
r	s	t	u	v	y
z	æ	ø			

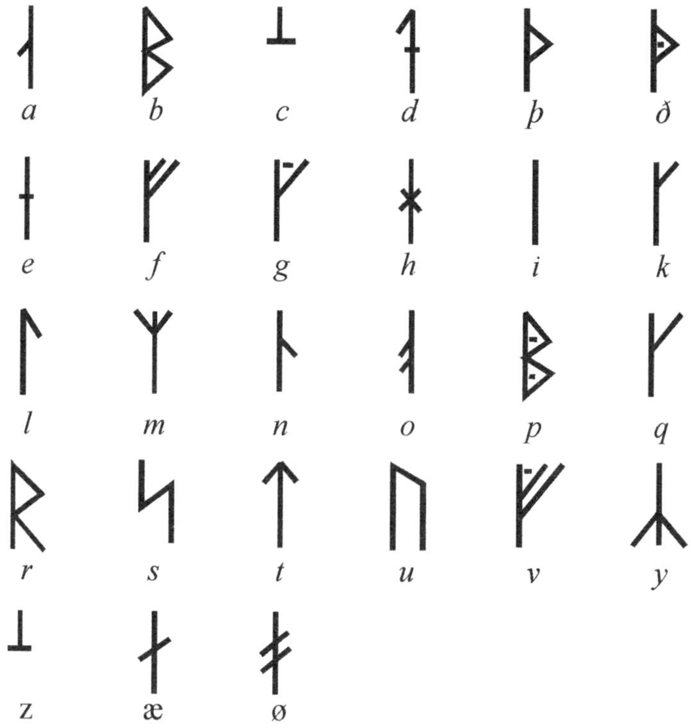

Extracts

The Lay of Sigrdrifa

Baldur's Dream

Hávamál: The Sayings of Hár

ᚠᚢᚦᚨᚱᚲᚷᚹ ᚺᚾᛁᛃᛇ
ᛈᛉᛊᛏᛒᛖᛗᛚᛜᛟᛞ

The Lay of Sigrdrifa

Sea runes you should know to save from wreck
Sail steeds on the Sea:
Carve them on the bow and the blade of the rudder,
Etch them with fire on the oars;
Though high the breakers and blue the waves.
You shall sail safe into harbour.

Limb-runes you should know if a leech you would be,
Who can properly probe wounds:
It is best to carve them on the bark of trees
Whose limbs lean to the east.

Speech-runes you should know, so that no man
Out of hatred may do you harm:
These you shall wind" these you shall fold,
These you shall gather together,
When the people throng to the Thing to hear
Just judgements given.

Thought-runes you should know if you would be thought by all
The wisest of mortal men:
Hropt devised them,
Hropt scratched them
Hropt took them to heart
From the wise waters the waters then run
From the head of Heidraupnir
From the horn of Hoddrofnir.

On the Ben he stood with Brimir's sword"
A helmet upon his head:
Then Mimir's head uttered for the first time
Words of great wisdom.

He spoke runes on the shied that stands before the shining god,
In the ear of Early Awake and on the hoof of All-Wise
On the wheel that turns ever under Hrungnir's chariot,
On the sled straps and on Sleipnir's teeth.

On the bears paw and on Bragi's tongue,
On the wolfs foot and the falcons beak,
On the bloody wings and at the bridges end,
On the palm of child loosener and the path of comfort .

On glass and on gold and the fore-guesses of men,
In wine and in malt and in the mind's seat,
On Gungnir's point and on Grani's breast,
On the nails of the Norns and the Night Owls beak.

All were scratched off which were scratched on,
Mingled with holy mead
And sent on the wide ways,
Some to gods some to elves,
Some to the wise Vanes,
Some to the sons of men

There are Beech runes, there are Birth Runes,
And all the ale runes
Precious runes of power!
Unspoiled they are un-spoiled they are,
Learn them and use them long
Till the high powers perish.

Now you shall choose, for the choice is given you,
Maple - of - well - forged - weapons,
Speech or silence, you shall say which:
Evil is allotted to all.

I shall not flee, though fated to die,
For never have I known fear.
Grant me but this give me all
Your love counsel while I live."

Baldur's Dream

The gods hurried to their hall of council,
Gathered together, goddesses with them,
All-powerful, eager to unriddle
Baldur's dream that such dread portended.

Up rose Odhinn, unaging magician,
Harnesses Sleipnir, the eight-legged,
Sped down from Asgard to Hel's Deep.

The blood-dabbled hound of Hel faced him,
Howling in frenzy at the father of runes.
The High One halted at the eastern gate,
Where loomed a tumulus, tomb of a witch.
Runes he chanted, charms of power:
Her spectre rose whom his spell commanded
To enlighten the god with the lore of the dead.

Balder Dead

"His own house Breidablik, on whose columns Balder graved
The enchantments that recall the dead to life.
For wise he was, and many curious arts,
Postures of runes, and healing herbs he knew;
Unhappy! but that art he did not know,
To keep his own life safe and see the sun.

Mathew Arnold.

Hávamál:
The Sayings of Hár

Now is answered what you ask of the runes,
Graven by the gods,
Made by the All Father,
Sent by the powerful sage:
It. is best for man to remain silent.

For these things give thanks at nightfall:
The day gone, a guttered torch,
A sword tested, the troth of a maid,
Ice crossed, ale drunk.

Hew wood in wind-time, in fine weather sail,
Tell in the night-time tales to house-girls,
For too many eyes are open by day:
From a ship expect speed, from a shield, cover,
Keenness from a sword, but a kiss from a girl.

Drink ale by the hearth, over ice glide,
Buy a stained sword, buy a starving mare
To fatten at home: and fatten the watch-dog.

Trust not an acre early sown,
Nor praise a son too soon:
Weather rules the acre, wit the son,
Both are exposed to peril,

A snapping bow, a burning flame,
A grinning wolf, a grunting boar,
A raucous crow, a rootless tree,
A breaking wave, a boiling kettle,
A flying arrow, an ebbing tide,
A coiled adder, the ice of a night,
A bride's bed talk, a broad sword,
A bear's play, a prince' s children,
A witch' s welcome, the wit of a slave,
A sick calf, a corpse still fresh,
A brother's killer encountered upon
The highway a house half-burned,
A racing stallion who has wrenched a leg,
Are never safe: let no man trust them.

No man should trust a maiden's words,
Nor what a woman speaks:
Spun on a wheel were women's hearts,
In their breasts was implanted caprice,

To love a woman whose ways are false
Is like sledding over slippery ice
With unshod horses out of control,
Badly trained two-year-olds,
Or drifting rudderless on a rough sea,
Or catching a reindeer with a crippled hand
On a thawing hillside: think not to do it.

Naked I may speak now for I know both:
Men are treacherous too
Fairest we speak when falsest we think:
many a maid is deceived.

Gallantly shall he speak and gifts bring
Who wishes for woman's love:
praise the features of the fair girl,
Who courts well will conquer.

Never reproach another for his love:
It happens often enough

That beauty ensnares with desire the wise
While the foolish remain unmoved.

Never reproach the plight of another,
For it happens to many men:
Strong desire may stupefy heroes,
Dull the wits of the wise

The mind alone knows what is near the heart,
Each is his own judge:
The worst sickness for a wise man
Is to crave what he cannot enjoy.

So I learned when I sat in the reeds,
Hoping to have my desire:
Lovely was the flesh of that fair girl,
But nothing I hoped for happened.

I saw on a bed Billing's daughter,
Sun white, asleep:
No greater delight I longed for then
Than to lie in her lovely arms.

"Come" Odhinn, after nightfall
If you wish for a meeting with me:
All would be lost if anyone saw us
And learned that we were lovers."

Afire with longing" I left her then,
Deceived by her soft words:
I thought my wooing had won the maid,
That I would have my way.

After nightfall I hurried back,
But the warriors were all awake,
Lights were burning, blazing torches:
So false proved the path

Towards daybreak back I came
The guards were sound asleep:
I found then that the fair woman
Had tied a bitch to her bed.

Many a girl when one gets to know her
Proves to be fickle and false:
That treacherous maiden taught me a lesson,
The crafty woman covered me with shame"
That was all I got from her.

Let a man with his guests be glad and merry,
Modest a man should be"
But talk well if he intends to be wise
And expects praise from men:
Fimbul fambi is the fool called "
Unable to open his mouth.
Fruitless my errand, had I been silent
When I came to Suttung's courts:
With spirited words I spoke to my profit
In the hall of the aged giant.

Rati had gnawed a narrow passage,
Chewed a channel through stone,
A path around the roads of giants:
I was like to lose my head

Gunnlod sat me in the golden seat,
Poured me precious mead:
Ill reward she had from me for that,
For her proud and passionate heart,
Her brooding foreboding spirit.

What I won from her I have well used:
I have waxed in wisdom since I came back,
bringing to Asgard Odrerir,
the sacred draught.

Hardly would I have come home alive
From the garth of the grim troll,

Had Gunnlod not helped me, the good woman,
Who wrapped her arms around me.

The following day the Frost Giants came,
Walked into Har's hall To ask for Har's advice:
Had Bolverk they asked, come back to his friends,
Or had he been slain by Suttung?

Odhinn, they said, swore an oath on his ring:
Who from now on will trust him?
By fraud at the feast he befuddled Suttung
And brought grief to Gunnlod.

It is time to sing in the seat of the wise,
Of what at Urd's Well I saw in silence,
saw and thought on.
Long I listened to men
Runes heard spoken, (counsels revealed.)
At Har's hall, In Har's hall:
There I heard this.

Loddfafnir, listen to my counsel:
You will fare well if you follow it,
It will help you much if you heed it.

Never rise at night unless you need to spy
Or to ease yourself in the outhouse.

Shun a woman, wise in magic,
Her bed and her embraces:
If she cast a spell, you will care no longer
To meet and speak with men,
Desire no food, desire no pleasure,
In sorrow fall asleep.

Never seduce anothers wife,
Never make her your mistress.

If you must journey to mountains and firths,
Take food and fodder with you.

Never open your heart to an evil man
When fortune does not favour you:
From an evil man, if you make him your friend,
You will get evil for good.

I saw a warrior wounded fatally
By the words of an evil woman
Her cunning tongue caused his death,
Though what she alleged was a lie.

If you know a friend you can fully trust,
Go often to his house
Grass and brambles grow quickly
Upon the untrodden track.

With a good man it is good to talk,
Make him your fast friend:
But waste no words on a witless oaf,
Nor sit with a senseless ape.

Cherish those near you, never be
The first to break with a friend:
Care eats him who can no longer
Open his heart to another.

An evil man, if you make him your friend,
Will give you evil for good:
A good man, if you make him your friend"
Will praise you in every place,

Affection is mutual when men can open
All their heart to each other:
He whose words are always fair
Is untrue and not to be trusted.

Bandy no speech with a bad man:
Often the better is beaten
In a word fight by the worse.

Be not a cobbler nor a carver of shafts,
Except it be for yourself:
If a shoe fit ill or a shaft be crooked"
The maker gets curses and kicks.

If aware that another is wicked, say so:
Make no truce or treaty with foes.

Never share in the shamefully gotten,
But allow yourself what is lawful.

Never lift your eyes and look up in battle,
Lest the heroes enchant you,
who can change warriors
Suddenly into hogs,
With a good woman, if you wish to enjoy
Her words and her good will,
Pledge her fairly and be faithful to it:
Enjoy the good you are given,

Be not over wary, but wary enough,
First, of the foaming ale,
Second, of a woman wed to another,
Third, of the tricks of thieves.

Mock not the traveller met On the road,
Nor maliciously laugh at the guest:
Scoff not at guests nor to the gate chase them,
But relieve the lonely and wretched,

The sitters in the hall seldom know
The kin of the new-comer:
The best man is marred by faults,
The worst is not without worth.

Never laugh at the old when they offer counsel,
Often their words are wise:
From shrivelled skin, from scraggy things
That hand among the hides
And move amid the guts,
Clear words often come.

Heavy the beam above the door;
Hang a horse-shoe On it
Against ill-luck, lest it should suddenly
Crash and crush your guests.

Medicines exist against many evils:
Earth against drunkenness, heather against worms
Oak against costiveness, corn against sorcery,
Spurred rye against rupture, runes against bales
The moon against feuds, fire against sickness,
Earth makes harmless the floods.

Wounded I hung on a wind-swept gallows
For nine long nights,
Pierced by a spear, pledged to Odhinn,
Offered, myself to myself
The wisest know not from whence spring
The roots of that ancient rood

They gave me no bread,
They gave me no mead,
I looked down;
with a loud cry I took up runes;
from that tree I fell.

Nine lays of power
I learned from the famous Bolthor, Bestla' s father:
He poured me a draught of precious mead,

Mixed with magic Odrerir.

Waxed and throve well;
Word from word gave words to me,
Deed from deed gave deeds to me,

Runes you will find, and readable staves,
Very strong staves,
Very stout staves,
Staves that Bolthor stained,
Made by mighty powers,
Graven by the prophetic god,

For the gods by Odhinn, for the elves by
Dain,
By Dvalin, too, for the dwarves,
By Asvid for the hateful giants,
And some I carved myself:
Thund, before man was made,
scratched them,
Who rose first, fell thereafter

Know how to cut them, know how to
read them,
Know how to stain them, know how to
prove them,
Know how to evoke them, know how
to score them,
Know how to send them" know how to
send them,

Odin

Pentacle Enterprises Books Available from Mandragora